SHAPED BY SCRIPTURE

More than Conquerors

ROMANS 8–16

DOUG WARD

Copyright © 2024 by The Foundry Publishing®
The Foundry Publishing
PO Box 419527
Kansas City, MO 64141
thefoundrypublishing.com

978-0-8341-4301-2

2

Cover Design: J. R. Caines
Interior Layout: Jeff Gifford

The internet addresses, email addresses, and phone numbers in this book are accurate at the time of publication. They are provided as a resource. The Foundry Publishing does not endorse them or vouch for their content or permanence.

Contents

Introduction to the *Shaped by Scripture* Series   4

Introduction to the Book of Romans   7

Week One: Life in the Spirit (Romans 8:1–17)   16

Week Two: The Fate of the World (Romans 8:18–39)   28

Week Three: Addressing Unbelief (Romans 9–10)   42

Week Four: All Will Be Saved (Romans 11)   56

Week Five: Practicing the Faith (Romans 12)   70

Week Six: When in Rome (Romans 13–14)   85

Week Seven: Unity Is the Key (Romans 15–16)   98

THE *SHAPED BY SCRIPTURE* SERIES

The first step of an organized study of the Bible is the selection of a biblical book, which is not always an easy task. Often people pick a book they are already familiar with, books they think will be easy to understand, or books that, according to popular opinion, seem to have more relevance to Christians today than other books of the Bible. However, it is important to recognize the truth that God's Word is not limited to just a few books. All the biblical books, both individually and collectively, communicate God's Word to us. As Paul affirms in 2 Timothy 3:16, "All Scripture is God-breathed and is useful for teaching, rebuking, correcting and training in righteousness." We interpret the term "God-breathed" to mean inspired by God. If Christians are going to take 2 Timothy 3:16 seriously, then we should all set the goal of encountering God's Word as communicated through all sixty-six books of the Bible. New Christians or those with little to no prior knowledge of the Bible might find it best to start with a New Testament book like 1 John, James, or the Gospel of John.

By purchasing this volume, you have chosen to study the second half of the book of Romans, which is considered by some to be Paul's greatest theological treatise. This epistle heavily emphasizes the reign of Christ and the role of faith in a believer's life.

How This Study Works

This Bible study is intended for a period of seven weeks. We have chosen a specific passage for each week's study. This study can be done individually or with a small group.

For individual study, we recommend a five-day study each week, following the guidelines given below:

1	On the first day of the study, read the relevant passage several times until you become fully familiar with the verses, words, and phrases.
2	On the second day, we will review the setting and organization of the passage.
3	On the third day, we will observe some of the realities portrayed in the passage.
4	On the fourth day, we will investigate the relationship of the individual passage to the larger story of God in the Bible.
5	On the fifth day, we will reflect on the function of the story as we hear it today, the invitation it extends to us, and our response to God, who speaks through God's Word.

If this Bible study is done as a group activity, we recommend that members of the group meet together on the sixth day to share and discuss what they have learned from God's Word and how it has transformed their lives.

You may want to have a study Bible to give you additional insights as we work through the book of Romans. Other helpful resources are *Discovering the New Testament* and the New Beacon Bible Commentary volumes *Romans 1–8* and *Romans 9–16*, available from The Foundry Publishing.

Literary Forms in the Bible

There are several literary forms represented throughout the Bible. The divinely inspired writers used various techniques to communicate God's Word to their ancient audiences. The major literary forms (also known as genres) of the Bible are:

- narratives

- laws

- history

- Wisdom literature (in the form of dialogues and proverbial statements)

- poetry (consisting of poems of praise, lament, trust in God, and more)

- prophecy

- discourses

- parables

- miracle stories

- letters (also known as epistles)

- exhortations

- apocalyptic writings

Within each of these forms, one may find subgenres. Each volume in the *Shaped by Scripture* series will briefly overview the genres found in the book of the Bible that is the subject of that study.

When biblical writers utilized a particular literary form, they intended for it to have a specific effect on their audience. This concept can be understood by examining genres that are familiar to us in our contemporary setting. For example, novels that are comedies inspire good and happy feelings in their readers; tragedies, on the other hand, are meant to induce sorrow. What is true of the intended effect of literary forms in contemporary literature is also true of literary forms found in the Bible.

THE BOOK OF ROMANS

The book of Romans is part of a larger collection of thirteen New Testament letters that have been attributed to the apostle Paul. The authorship of six of these letters is debated to some extent today. Three (1 Timothy, Titus, and 2 Thessalonians) are considered by many scholars to be doubtful in their connection to Paul. Three others (Colossians, Ephesians, and 2 Timothy) are disputed by some, although the trend is swinging back toward Pauline authorship. The seven that remain (Galatians, 1 and 2 Corinthians, Romans, 1 Thessalonians, Philippians, and Philemon) are widely considered to be undisputed letters from the hand of Paul.

Among these seven letters, Romans clearly stands apart. Paul's letter to the church in Rome is the jewel of Pauline literature. It is the letter where we see the most complete expression of Pauline theology and practice. In it we can see the depth and breadth of Paul's thought and his deep concern for this new faith.

In most of his letters, Paul is responding to an ongoing issue in the church to whom the letter is written. Sometimes that local church has written to Paul with a list of questions they have about congregational problems or theological issues (see 1 Corinthians). In other letters, Paul is emotionally responding to a sudden crisis that needs his immediate attention (see Galatians). In still others, Paul is writing a personal letter to a person he knows well (see Philemon).

None of these reasons for writing are present in Romans. In this letter Paul is writing to a church he did not start and has never visited in person but would like to visit in the near future. He wants to introduce himself to the church and allow the church to get to know him and the gospel message he proclaims. In Romans, Paul has time to think about what is important, so he takes his time and presents his argument in a lengthy and orderly fashion.

Romans, more than any other letter, is a glimpse into the mind and theology of Paul. Perhaps for this reason, Romans has always been a highly important New Testament work, especially for those in the Protestant world. Martin Luther considered Romans to be the central part of the New Testament, while John Calvin said it opened a gateway for the rest of the Bible. John Wesley was reading Luther's "Preface to Romans" when he felt his heart strangely warmed. It would not be an exaggeration to say that Romans has been the most influential book in the New Testament when it comes to the theology of the church. Within the pages of this letter, one finds the problem of

7

humanity explained, God's response to the problem we created, and how the Christian life is to be lived. Romans is Paul's thorough presentation of what it means to be a Christian.

Who Wrote Romans?

Romans was undeniably written by the apostle Paul. When some people think about Paul, they have an image of this leader of the early church confidently advising these young congregations in a difficult environment. The biggest problem with that view is that Paul was never recognized as a leader of the early church. He openly flouted the rules and expectations of the leadership of the church in Jerusalem. As a result, Jerusalem's leadership never trusted him, and some in the Jewish wing of the early Christian church actively opposed his efforts. To them, Paul was a dangerous presence, opening the church to gentiles without requiring them to fully observe the Jewish requirements.

Many believers today fail to appreciate how difficult the battle was for Paul. Before his encounter with Christ on the road to Damascus, he spent considerable time and energy persecuting the first Jewish believers in the early church. His motive was to keep the Jewish faith pure and the synagogue free from controversy and improper belief. Proclaiming that a crucified Jesus was their Messiah was intolerable for Saul. After his dramatic experience on the Damascus road, Paul changed his stripes and tried to integrate with the early church. Understandably, those efforts did not go well. Few were willing to trust a former leading persecutor of the church. He eventually found an ally in the church at Antioch—a congregation that accepted Paul, befriended him, supported his ministry, and sent him on his missionary journeys.

Early in his ministry, he was on the opposite side of the question of gentile inclusion from Peter and James. Paul passionately believed gentiles could be full participants in the new faith without being required to observe Jewish customs. Paul's biggest challenge was in trying to convince the early church to trust him and not James, the very *brother* of Jesus, or Peter, Jesus's own disciple. The fact that so many of Paul's letters remain demonstrate to us that his view eventually carried the day, but in the first century, the issue was very much in doubt.

Although the issue was murky in the collective opinion of the early church, it was exceedingly clear to Paul. Jesus commanded his followers to make disciples of every nation. "Every nation" includes gentiles! Requiring new believers to become Jewish first would make Jesus's command meaningless, and the early church would never have become "Christianity" but would have remained a faction of Judaism forever. The tension between Jewish and gentile Christianity persisted throughout Paul's entire ministry, but it was not the only tension the early church experienced. These early believers existed within the larger Roman Empire. The largest and most powerful nation the world had ever known was at the height of its power and influence in the first century, and Rome was its capital city. To reach the world that existed then, Christians in Rome would need a thriving local church that directed people to Christ. Paul wanted his influence to be known in that church.

Literary Form

Romans, like the other Pauline literature in the New Testament, is a letter, but the subject matter is so widespread that it lacks the focus of a personal letter, or of one like Galatians that targets a specific issue. Even so, there are well-recognized traits of an ancient letter in Romans. The usual epistolary greeting is prominent, as is the concluding section filled with personal notes and greetings. Romans also probably has the most noted *paraenesis* of the New Testament letters. A *paraenesis* is the section of a letter where the writer gives practical advice on how to respond based on what is presented in the main body of the letter. Romans 12–14 is a wonderful example of a *paraenesis*.

In recent years scholars have noted the presence and importance of a style known as diatribe within Paul's letter to the Romans. When we hear that word today, we often imagine an intense argument or a scuffle between two opponents. In ancient rhetoric, however, this word is used differently. In Romans, Paul is often arguing not with a specific opponent but against anticipated objections to his statements. His effective use of rhetorical diatribe shows that he is engaged in an important teaching dialogue with Christian Jews and gentiles about this new faith that is connected to Judaism but also stands apart in many critical ways.

The reader of Romans should also be aware of blocks of material that thematically connect. Romans 1–3, 5–8, and 9–11 are examples of sections that need to be read as a larger block of material and understood together.

Date

Romans is one of the New Testament books where we can confidently get close to the date of composition. Paul wrote Romans during his third missionary journey, what some scholars have called his "letter-writing journey." In his third journey, Paul retraced his steps from his second journey. Paul's second journey was noteworthy due to its length, his entrance into Europe, and because Luke joined him in the middle of it. That is where the account in Acts changes from the third person to a first-person description (16:9). Much of what we know about Paul is due to Luke joining this journey and later writing about the events that transpired.

Paul's second journey lasted from 49 to 53 CE. During that trip, Paul traveled extensively through Greece and stayed in Corinth for an extended period of eighteen months. Corinth was a great place for Paul to evangelize because it was a cultural hub of Graeco-Roman society in the first century. It was located on the narrow peninsula separating mainland Greece from the Peloponnesian peninsula. As a result of its location, Corinth was a city with seaports on either end of the town, and goods were transported overland between the two ports, saving time from having to sail around the entire peninsula. This feature made Corinth a hub of trade and transportation. It also was the home of ten pagan temples, making it a center for religious tourism and observance. Corinth also was a young and vibrant city, having been established fewer than a hundred years previously, so it was growing and had become a destination for recently freed slaves. If there was a new idea or philosophy one wanted to spread, it would be hard to find a better place than Corinth.

During his eighteen-month stay, Paul made numerous friends and was a fixture at the young church that met there. Among the people in Corinth were a Jewish couple displaced from Rome named Priscilla and Aquila. In 54 this couple moved back to Rome. Paul returned from this journey in 53 and embarked on his third journey a year later. From 54 to 57, Paul traveled around the empire again, largely to cities he had already visited. Paul wanted to see how these churches were doing and encourage them. In roughly 56 CE, Paul made his way back to the familiar community of Corinth. It was a comfortable place for him, and he decided while there to write a letter to the church in Rome. In the familiar environs of Corinth, Paul wrote what he considered to be important. He hoped to make it to Rome and meet the church someday. If he could get the gospel to the capital city of the empire, there would be no place where the gospel could not go.

Entering the Story

In roughly the first half of Romans, Paul has been addressing a church where division is present between Jews and gentiles and has been threatening to develop into a deeper divide. After the banishment of the Jews from Rome, the church became dominated by the gentiles who remained behind. The crowning of a new emperor in 54 led to the Jewish ban being lifted and the early Jewish believers returning to the city and the church they had left behind. However, the church they returned to was different than the church they had left. It had become gentile in composition, perhaps also in operation. When the early Jewish believers returned, they were in the minority and perhaps felt marginalized in the church they once called home.

Paul spent the early chapters of Romans sometimes addressing the Jewish believers and other times addressing the gentiles. His intent was to show both groups that sin impacts all of us equally and that all people are in need of the grace of Jesus Christ.

On the political side, there was hope that things would be better under the new emperor, Nero, than they were under Claudius's difficult reign, which saw secret trials, frequent executions, and the banishment of the Jews. Nero made many promises to bring a more fair and open governing style. The secret trials of Claudius were largely stopped, but Nero's mother, who had been Claudius's wife, was active behind the scenes and killed a few prominent opponents early in Nero's reign. We cannot say for certain if there were early signs of the unstable ruler and reign that were to come under Nero's control, but the church in Rome was always in a precarious position. Believers had to be mindful.

Historical Setting

Romans shows the extent of Paul's thought and theology. Paul did not come to his opinions haphazardly but only after a long period of reflection and struggle in the aftermath of what happened to him in Damascus. Paul spent the first part of his life dedicated to the study of the law and of practicing correct behavior. As a youth, he was a dedicated and driven student in Jerusalem under Gamaliel, and as an adult he traveled to problem synagogues correcting doctrinal issues. He was on his way to Damascus in this role when his life was suddenly changed on a dusty road by an encounter with Jesus Christ.

This encounter changed everything for Paul, and not immediately for the better. We know the first part of the story. Paul was blinded, weakened by his ordeal, and hiding from his former Jewish compatriots. We might think the newly reoriented Paul immediately started a public ministry proclaiming his new faith in Christ, but that is not what happened. After some early sermons in Damascus, Paul was forced into a period of long inactivity due to his unique circumstances but also because he needed time to process his new experience. As a man who loved ideas and intellectual debate, these years were probably the hardest for Paul. He was shunned by his former fellow Jewish leaders. He had left for Damascus to bring order in a synagogue where some were proclaiming Christ as the crucified and risen Messiah. A few days later, the former disciplinarian was a believer in Christ himself. Paul's career among these Jewish leaders was suddenly and unexpectedly over.

Unfortunately, he was not trusted by the early church either because they had only known him as Saul, persecutor of the new church. Trust took a long time to take hold. We do not know exactly when Paul began to follow Christ, but somewhere around 30–33 CE is likely. We do know he began his first journey in roughly 47, making a gap of around fifteen years between his encounter of Jesus on the road to Damascus and his initial efforts in Antioch. During this time, Paul read his beloved Scriptures, trying to make sense of everything. Meeting the resurrected Christ meant Paul had to reexamine everything.

Eventually, through the help of Barnabas, Paul became part of the church in Antioch—the church that sent him on his first missionary journey. His journey attracted the attention of the church in Jerusalem, who responded by sending representatives after Paul in an effort to correct his theological excesses. The church in Jerusalem heard Paul was allowing gentiles into the church as full participants without observing the law, and they thought that was a dangerous precedent that could not go uncorrected.

In Antioch, everything began to make sense again for Paul. Paul had formerly valued the law above everything else and thought it was the central expression of God's purposes in the world. When Paul met Christ, he was forced to admit this event had nothing to do with the law he defended so vigorously, so he scrambled to find a role for the law and a new central principle to take the law's place. In Antioch, Paul saw the gentiles experience the same Christ he had. If gentiles experienced what he had, then the law could not be the pinnacle of faith.

In place of the law, Paul found a new power that replaced his former zeal for the law. Happily for Paul, this new animating force in the church could be found right in the middle of his beloved Hebrew Scriptures. What was happening in Antioch had been prominent in his beloved Judaism for centuries—the Spirit had been poured out. Men and women, Jews and gentiles, slaves and free had all experienced the risen Christ, as Joel 2:28 had prophesied. The Spirit promised in Jeremiah 31:31–34 and Ezekiel 37:14 had been poured out on all flesh, and everything had decisively changed. It took Paul years to work all of this out. Since he had time in Corinth, he wanted to record his new understanding, and the letter to Rome was the perfect opportunity. The Spirit is the answer to Paul's anguished cry at the end of chapter 7. As the latter half of Romans begins, the Spirit will take center stage.

There remains an incorrect belief among Christians that God changed Saul's name to Paul after his encounter of Christ on the Damascus road. In fact, for all of his life, his name was Saulus Paulus of Tarsus, following the Roman custom of a tribal (ethnic) name, followed by a Romanized version and the town of one's birth. When Saul was in Jerusalem, people naturally called him Saul. On his missionary trips, he was called Paul. When he returned to Jerusalem in Acts 20, he was Saul again. For the rest of this study, he will be Paul.

Context of the Letter

In the first half of Romans, Paul felt compelled to teach the church about the problem facing humanity. For many Jewish believers, the problem was made clear by gentiles: they worshiped false gods and did not possess the law to guide them. There was hope for the gentiles, but they would have to worship the Jewish God and become Jewish in practice. The resurrection of the Jewish Messiah did not change their feelings about gentiles. Yes, Jesus may have died for everyone, but the Jews were still the chosen people, and if the benefits of the resurrection were to be applied, each person needed to be Jewish first.

Paul changed this expectation and began to plant churches where Jewish and gentile believers were equal in every way—a revolutionary approach, and cause for concern in the Jewish-led church in Jerusalem. After Paul preached in an area proclaiming simple faith as the standard for membership in the church, leaders from Jerusalem would go to that same area and proclaim the requirement of circumcision and the other Jewish laws. Paul saw this behavior as denying the monotheism of God. If they were forcing gentiles to be Jews in order to worship God, then necessarily that meant God was only God of the Jews. If Jews wanted to proclaim God as God of the whole world, then gentiles must be allowed to be fully part of God's family without imposing Jewish conversion or restrictions on them.

These key points are what got Paul in so much trouble with Jewish leadership. To their minds, Paul devalued them, their traditions, and the law. In case these accusations had reached the church in Rome, Paul used his letter to the Roman church to respond to these criticisms. The *Romans 1–7* volume in this series covers those chapters in great detail.

Any reader of Romans should understand that chapters 5–8 naturally fit together, so when we start this study with chapter 8, we ought to remember we are nearing the end of a larger section. Even so, the tone at the beginning of chapter 8 changes from the anguish that ends chapter 7, offering a natural breaking point and a good place to begin a study of the latter half of the epistle.

Paul's confidence in the dynamic presence of the Spirit in our lives is the hope of the world. The good news is that Jews and gentiles alike can fully experience God's grace.

More particularly for the believers in Rome, Paul wanted to answer the question: *How do God's people live in a culture that is hostile to the faith?* Rome was immensely powerful, and those who believed in Christ were not. Around two years before Romans was written, Nero had taken the throne. While we cannot be sure what events transpired to give an indication of what was to come, Paul's discerning mind may have seen some early hints of trouble. The church would have to navigate the Roman world carefully. Believers in *every* culture have to be careful. Romans offers both ancient and modern readers great advice on this topic as well.

Major Theological Themes

Romans, as Paul's most extensive and systematic treatise about God and this new faith that eventually came to be called Christianity, is rich with theological themes we will explore together over the next few weeks.

Life according to the flesh leads to death, while life according to the Spirit leads to abundant life and resurrection.

Concepts of the Trinity are prevalent in Romans even though Paul didn't use that language.

We are able to hope in the resurrection because of the aid and intercession of the Holy Spirit on our behalf.

God does not cause bad things to happen to us but is capable of using evil for his purpose and glory.

God chooses God's people to partner with God in bringing God's blessing, salvation, redemption, and hope of resurrection to the entire world.

God's love is so immense and powerful that we cannot be separated from it by anything or anyone.

God is patient and merciful because of God's great love for us.

Spiritual gifts are various, numerous, do not exist in a hierarchy of importance, and are given by God to us for humble service to the church.

Unity and love in the church are more important than individual judgment of the convictions of other believers.

Division in the church undermines the witness of the church to the world.

ROMANS 8:1-17

The church in Rome was in a unique position. It had a front-row seat for viewing the machinations of the most powerful nation the world had ever seen. The church in Rome would come into contact with various powerful people and governing authorities. If the rulers in Rome ever turned on the church, the Christians in Rome would be the first to suffer. It was a precarious position but one with opportunities as well. Paul hoped to make it to Rome and meet the members of this church in person. Before that happened, Paul wanted to write a letter, introduce himself, and present his gospel to this young church. Paul saw the importance of the church in Rome and wanted to ensure that their presentation of the gospel would be effective.

Paul spent the first half of Romans presenting the problem that all of humanity shares—the grinding presence of sin. The problem of sin dominated the Roman world and its capital. Politically, Rome sought to conquer the world, and the methods they used left death and destruction in their wake. The games presented for the populace featured and celebrated death, and the cheering of the crowds demonstrated a callous disregard for life. The presence of pagan temples and the loose morality that permeated Rome only completed the picture of a society completely disconnected from God. This sinful culture was not a gentile problem alone, and Paul firmly included the Jews in his presentation of sin run amok in chapters 1–7. It was a bleak picture.

In chapter 8, Paul is ready to present an alternative and hope-filled option to believers in Christ.

WEEK 1, DAY 1

Absorb the passage in Romans 8:1–17 by reading it aloud several times until you become familiar with its verses, words, and phrases.

WEEK 1, DAY 2
ROMANS 8:1-17

The Setting

We cannot appreciate the words of chapter 8 unless we remember where Paul left the readers of his letter at the end of chapter 7. He ultimately ends chapter 7 in a hopeless place. He reminded the believers that any attempt to build their faith around the law was futile. Try as even the most dedicated followers might, the law could not impart righteousness—that was never its purpose. The law was given to identify sin. Speaking as a representative of all who tried to live according to the law, Paul wrote an impassioned presentation of the problem. When we know what the law states, sin uses that knowledge to create in us a desire to do what is wrong. The law identifies our sin and tells us that we stand outside of what God desires. It is a cycle of condemnation for the law keeper. Paul realized this and cried out, "Who will rescue me from this body that is subject to death?" (7:24).

The Message

Chapter 8, as Paul's long-awaited answer to the problem of sin, is easily the climax of this letter to the Romans. It may even be the theological climax of the entire New Testament. Paul's answer clearly rings out to the church that God has not left us alone and has provided a living answer to our problem of sin and death. There is a surprise in chapter 8 for readers who expect to find a long treatise on how the cross of Christ changed everything. While that is under the surface, it is not Paul's explicit answer. For Paul, the answer to sin is a daily walk with the Holy Spirit, who gives life to the believer. The Spirit is not an afterthought in Romans. The Spirit is God's answer to a world that needs to be set straight again.

To discover the message of Romans 8, let's divide the passage into four sections. **Summarize the general message or theme of each section.**

1. Romans 8:1–4

_____

_____

_____

_____

_____

_____

2. Romans 8:5–8

_____

_____

_____

_____

_____

_____

_____

_____

3. Romans 8:9–11

_____

_____

_____

18

_____

_____

_____

_____

_____

_____

4. Romans 8:12–17

_____

_____

_____

_____

_____

_____

_____

_____

_____

WEEK 1, DAY 3

What's Happening in the Passage?

As we read through these passages there are certain ideas and words that were familiar to the original readers but are not as familiar to us. Two thousand years and a vastly different culture obscure some of these ideas from us today. You may encounter some of these words and ideas in your study today. Some of them have been explained in more detail in the **Word Study Notes** below. If you want even more detail you can supplement this study with a Bible dictionary or commentary.

1. Romans 8:1–4

The latter half of Romans begins with perhaps the most cele-bratory words of the entire New Testament, and they directly follow the dark closing of chapter 7. The purpose of the law[1] is to condemn sin, but that condemnation has been answered in the person of Jesus. The law produces a desire to do the exact thing it prohibits. When the law is used by the Spirit, it leads us to a knowledge of our need for redemption and drives us to Jesus Christ. The death and resurrection of Jesus create a new life that overcomes sin, and the ever-present Spirit enables and empow-ers the believer to live differently, which is something the law could never do. There is an interesting turn of phrase in verse 3. Through the cross, Jesus has *condemned sin in the flesh*.[2] Death was always the end result of sin's work, but when Jesus rose from the dead, the ultimate power of sin was publicly defeated. Because of this event the righteousness the law always pointed to but could not produce can now be lived by believers. Paul even tells the believers what it takes to initiate such a life: a daily walk with the Spirit.

2. Romans 8:5–8

Paul is purposefully presenting two conflicting ways to approach life and conduct. There is the way of the flesh and the way of the Spirit. When Paul describes those who live according to the flesh, he is not describing a life that focuses on sensual plea-sures. He is describing a life that is oriented toward satisfying any desire of the self. When food, money, power, or sex become the focus of life, we are living according to the flesh.[1]

WORD STUDY NOTES #1

[1] One important discussion is determining what Paul means when he uses the word "law." Most of the time in Romans it is clear, but in 8:2 his meaning is unclear. There are times when "law" means an impersonal force or power. Most of the time in Romans "law" means the covenant given to Moses at Sinai. This was Israel's special possession. Which meaning we give to "law" in 8:2 has implications with how we read the text.

[2] This is a direct reference to the humanity of Christ. Jesus walked among us, and the political and religious leaders of the day put him to death using the same law that some Jewish believers wished to elevate.

WORD STUDY NOTES #2

[1] "The flesh" refers to anything that tempts us into believing we are sovereign and free from God's direction.

WORD STUDY NOTES #3

[1] Some claim that the Bible has no basis for a doctrine of the Trinity because there is never any explicit mention or explication of it. These verses in Romans 8 have Trinitarian ideas front and center. Paul equates Christ with God and names the Spirit as an animating presence in the believer's life as well as the power that raised Christ from the dead.

[2] Life in the Spirit is made possible by the death and resurrection of Christ. Those who daily seek the Spirit know the joy of loving God, loving others, and the possibility of pursuing holiness.

[3] Paul knew he was addressing people who lived in the shadow of Rome. He was not promising problem-free living; he merely wanted to assure them that, even in a sin-dominated world, the Spirit would continually give life.

[4] The presence of the Spirit means that new life is a promise. If the Spirit of the risen Christ lives in us, we have the promise of the resurrection in us as well.

WORD STUDY NOTES #4

[1] There are times when the outcome guaranteed by the presence of the Spirit can seem hidden to believers. At these times we should remember that the Spirit gave life to Jesus at the resurrection and that life is promised to us as well.

[2] "Abba, Father" could be a reference to the words of Jesus in Gethsemane. It could also be a reference to Genesis. Abraham plays a large role in Paul's train of thought in Romans. Both Isaac and Ishmael were physical descendants of Abraham, but only Isaac was the son of the promise. Abraham's family includes more than the physical descendants. The gentiles were a part of the original promise to Abraham.

Create your own brief summary or description of the reality portrayed in verses 9–11.

3. Romans 8:9–11[1, 2, 3, 4]

_____

_____

_____

_____

_____

_____

_____

_____

_____

_____

_____

_____

4. Romans 8:12–17

We have a choice: we can live according to the flesh or according to the Spirit. The problem with flesh is that it is always dying. It leads to decisions and outcomes that lead to diminished life and degrading relationships. You can adorn the flesh with the power and grandeur of Rome, but it does not change the reality of death. The Spirit, however, leads to life.[1] Paul encourages the gentile believers, reminding them that they are fully part of God's family as children of God whom God has adopted—which is why we can call God "Abba, Father."[2] Paul also insists that being children of God makes us co-heirs with Christ, who is also God's child. There is no false promise to be spared from suffering; instead, Paul says we can expect to suffer and also to share in Christ's glory.

Discoveries

Let's summarize our discoveries from Romans 8:1–17.

1. Romans 8 offers the light of hope to the darkness of Romans 7.

2. Living according to the flesh will lead to death while life by the Spirit leads to true life and resurrection.

3. We have a choice about which kind of life we want to live.

4. The world is tainted with sin, and following Jesus won't change that reality, but life in the Spirit gives us hope.

5. Being children of God means we follow the path of Jesus toward suffering, resurrection, and glory.

If you have a study Bible, it may have references in a margin, a middle column, or footnotes that point to other biblical texts. You may find it helpful in understanding

how the whole story of God ties together to look up some of those other scriptures from time to time.

The Spirit and the Story of God

Whenever we read a biblical text, it is important to ask how the text we are reading relates to the rest of the Bible. Romans 8 is not the only place in the Bible where the Spirit is emphasized and promised.

In the space provided, write a short summary of how the Spirit changes the lives of people in other parts of Scripture.

1. Jeremiah 31:31–34

_____

_____

_____

_____

_____

_____

_____

_____

2. Ezekiel 36:25–27

_____

_____

_____

_____

_____

_____

_____

3. John 14:15–31

4. Galatians 5:13–26

5. Revelation 22:12–21

WEEK 1, DAY 5

Romans and Our World Today

When we consider the theme of life in the Spirit, we can see remarkable parallels to our own day and time. Romans 8 can become the lens through which we see ourselves, our world, and how God works in our world today.

1. How should life in the Spirit change the life of a believer?

When he talks about living according to the Spirit, Paul has in mind a directional quality to a believer's intention and life. We have a choice. We can either live each day depending on our human abilities and resources, or we can live each day intentionally depending on the Spirit's immense resources. Life in the Spirit requires a whole-hearted orientation of will and character, not a perfection of execution.

Following the above example, answer these questions about how we can understand ourselves, our world, and God's action in our world today.

2. If we believe there is no condemnation for us, why do so many Christians today still struggle with guilt and shame?

_____

_____

_____

_____

_____

3. How do Christians today still try to live according to the law instead of the Spirit?

_____

_____

_____

_____

_____

_____

4. Why does a Spirit-filled life feel like an unattainable goal to some?

_____

_____

_____

_____

_____

_____

_____

_____

_____

_____

_____

_____

_____

_____

5. How does our status as God's children change the way we think about our relationship with God?

_____

_____

_____

_____

_____

_____

_____

_____

_____

_____

_____

_____

_____

_____

Invitation and Response

God's Word always invites a response. Think about how the theme of life according to the Spirit speaks to us today. How does it invite us to respond?

Paul wants to make it clear that the believer has a choice to make. Because of what grace has accomplished, we can follow the Spirit. The believer has the Spirit-aided ability to say no to sin and yes to God. We also have the freedom to say no to God-which is why we need to pursue the Spirit daily. We live in a world that is still governed by sin and death, but with the Spirit we know that death will no longer write the last chapter of our lives. The Spirit fills us with new life that enables us to love, empowers us to serve, and keeps us from the degrading and diminishing effects of sin.

What is your evaluation of yourself based on any or all of the verses found in Romans 8:1–17?

Being children of God means we
follow the path of Jesus toward
suffering, resurrection, and glory.

ROMANS 8:18-39

Paul opened chapter 8 with the triumphant cry that believers are no longer subject to condemnation. This is the victory that we need from the problem of sin presented in the first half of the letter. This is truly good news, but Paul also cautions that we should expect to share in the sufferings of Christ. As we will read in this latter half of chapter 8, suffering is not reserved for only those under the thumb of Nero in Rome but is experienced by all of creation. Salvation, like sin, is not only an individual problem but also a cosmic one.

WEEK 2, DAY 1

Absorb the passage in Romans 8:18–39 by reading it aloud several times until you become familiar with its verses, words, and phrases.

WEEK 2, DAY 2

ROMANS 8:18-39

The Setting

Christians are well acquainted with their own personal struggles. Every single human is made in the image of God yet affected by the temptation to sin. Although we do not all have the same spiritual struggles, we do all have them in some form or other. Thankfully, the Holy Spirit enables us to be delivered from the power of sin. Even the most Spirit-filled believer recognizes how sin has impacted our world. We see its damage in our communities, we see the impact sin has on families, and we see sin wield its power through political entities around the world. It can be disheartening for any believer. We know God has an answer for our personal sins, but does God also have an answer for the damaged world?

The Message

Personal transgressions against God do not make up the totality of the extent of sin. Sin is also collective and social as well as individual. Communal sin is a reality even in parts of the world where relative comfort and wealth can at times hide the awful consequences of sin. Paul reminded the church in Rome of a truth that would not have been news to them: sin impacts the entire world. He wanted them to know that grace is the answer for corporate sin just as much as it is the answer to our individual sin.

To discover the message of Romans 8:18–39, let's divide the passage into six sections. **Summarize the general message or theme of each section (following the pattern provided for verses 26–27).**

1. Romans 8:18–21

2. Romans 8:22–25

_____

_____

_____

_____

_____

_____

_____

_____

3. Romans 8:26–27

Before he was crucified, Jesus promised to send an advocate to his disciples. That advocate was the Holy Spirit. Paul has taken that promise to heart, explaining in these verses exactly what kind of relationship we can have with the Spirit and how the Spirit can bring us closer to the heavenly Father.

_____

_____

_____

_____

4. Romans 8:28–30

_____

_____

_____

_____

_____

_____

_____

_____

5. Romans 8:31–34

6. Romans 8:35–39

WEEK 2, DAY 3

What's Happening in the Passage?

As we read through these passages there are certain ideas and words that were familiar to the original readers but are not as familiar to us. Two thousand years and a vastly
different culture obscure some of these ideas from us today. You may encounter some
of these words and ideas in your study today. Some of them have been explained in
more detail in the **Word Study Notes** below. If you want even more detail you can
supplement this study with a Bible dictionary or commentary.

1. Romans 8:18–21

Paul begins this passage with the hope that what is coming for the believer is greater than any hardship experienced in the world. This encouragement would be great
news for any church existing so close to the capital of Rome. Sin has not only impacted individual lives and communities but also all of creation. Creation awaits the action
of the church. If we fail to live out the resurrection life that the Spirit provides, the
damage is inflicted on the larger world.

**Create your own brief summary or description of the reality portrayed in verses
22–25.**

2. Romans 8:22–25

_____

_____

_____

_____

_____

3. Romans 8:26–27

When God's people are groaning, the Spirit groans with us. Our struggle does not
go unnoticed by an uncaring God. We have been given the Spirit, who is a guide and
comfort but is also our guarantee of the resurrection. Our pain is not meaningless,
and our lives serve a purpose. The Spirit is not distant from those who suffer. Instead,
the Spirit intercedes on our account. Our God is not impersonal or detached.

4. Romans 8:28

Paul answers the question of what intercession by the Spirit means with one of the most misquoted, misused, and misunderstood passages in the New Testament. Verse 28 does not tell believers that God causes bad things to happen just so God can bring something good from it. Verse 28 follows what has come before about the redemption of creation. There is a direction in our lives under the guidance of the Spirit, and that direction is toward resurrection. Bad things will happen to us because bad things happen to everyone. God does not *cause* bad things to happen, but Paul proclaims that when they do happen, we—with the Spirit's help—remain pointed toward our ultimate goal of being united with God in resurrection. People notice how we bear burdens. When God's people are hurting and weakened, others will note how the Spirit empowers us. The Spirit is so powerful that God can take evil and use it for his glory. God can use what was intended for evil for a larger good.[1]

5. Romans 8:29-30

Many read the word "predestined" in verse 29 and imagine a select group God has chosen to receive salvation.[1] A careful read of these verses shows this is not the case. God's relationship with the "predestined" is for the purpose of bringing God's salvation to the entire world.[2] The purpose of what God is doing is that Christ might be the firstborn of "many brothers and sisters." When God calls a people, it is done so that the world may be redeemed. God's plan will succeed because Christ is the sufficient means to accomplish his purpose.

WORD STUDY NOTES #4

[1] A number of prominent scholars have argued that Romans 8:28 has been slightly mistranslated. They say it should read, "in all things God works **with** the good of those who love him." If this meaning is primary, the meaning of the passage becomes more clear. In a world that is damaged by sin, God works *with* people to bring about the freedom of redemption. God has always worked with humanity to accomplish God's will. The church exists to partner with God in reversing the effects of sin.

WORD STUDY NOTES #5

[1] Thanks to the Reformed tradition, when we read the word "predestined" in Scripture today, we are tempted to think of it through the lens of John Calvin. In that tradition, God is said to have pre-selected a group of people for exclusive salvation. We should remember that a definition from the 1500s, old as it seems to us, is still much newer than the ancient text of Scripture. Paul and John Calvin did not have the same definition of predestination.

[2] When Paul uses the word "predestined," he is referring to the Jews as God's chosen people. We must remember that both the New Testament and the Old Testament proclaim that God's salvation is for all. The Jews were chosen to receive God's blessing in order that they might be the vessel through which the *world* receives God's blessing.

Create your own brief summary or description of the reality portrayed in verses 31–34.

6. Romans 8:31–34[1]

WORD STUDY NOTES #6

[1] Paul asks a question that purposefully echoes the opening cry of chapter 8 that there is no condemnation for those who are in Christ: "Who then is the one who condemns?" Paul's answer is "no one."

_____

_____

_____

_____

_____

_____

7. Romans 8:35–39

The church in Rome still lived in a dangerous time that was growing more antagonistic by the day. The threat of persecution was a real danger to the young church. Paul responds by writing one of the most moving promises of the Bible. He assures believers that there is nothing that can separate us from the love of God.[1] No trial in the present or worry about the future diminishes God's love. Because of God's love, no disease will ever be able to write the final chapter. And no penalty that Nero could ever impose can stop God's love either. The ultimate reality for the believer is the resurrection of Jesus Christ. Paul's words here are a simple reminder that we serve the greater power; therefore, we do not have to fear the lesser power, even when the lesser power appears very powerful to us.

WORD STUDY NOTES #7

[1] Paul's inclusion of "neither angels nor demons" has led some to attempt to imagine an unseen spiritual world where angels and demons battle over our lives. These speculative worlds lead to anxious thoughts over whether we are saying the right prayers to keep our divine protection. In such cases we become little more than pawns in greater heavenly struggles. Paul would frown at such speculation. His point is much simpler. He uses opposing concepts to demonstrate the breadth and completeness of God's provision for God's people.

Discoveries

Let's summarize our discoveries from Romans 8:18–39.

1. Our hope is in the resurrection.

2. We are able to hope in the resurrection because of the aid and intercession of the Holy Spirit on our behalf.

3. God does not cause bad things to happen to us but is capable of using evil for his purpose and glory.

4. Paul's use of the word "predestined" has a very different meaning than John Calvin's use of the same word.

5. God chooses God's people to partner with God in bringing God's blessing, salvation, redemption, and hope of resurrection to the entire world.

6. God's love is so immense and powerful that we cannot be separated from it by anything or anyone.

WEEK 2, DAY 4

The Fate of the World and the Story of God

Whenever we read a biblical text, it is important to ask how the text we are reading relates to the rest of the Bible. The latter half of Romans 8 is not the only place in the Bible where God's desire is described as changing the world. **In the space provided, write a short summary of how the fate of the world is prominent in other parts of Scripture and how God's presence changes outcomes.**

1. Joel 2:28–32

_____

_____

_____

_____

_____

_____

_____

2. Matthew 28:16–20

_____

_____

_____

_____

_____

_____

_____

_____

_____

_____

_____

3. Acts 10:30–48

_____

_____

_____

_____

_____

_____

_____

_____

4. Ephesians 3:1–10

_____

_____

_____

_____

_____

_____

_____

_____

37

5. Revelation 21:1–5

_____

_____

_____

_____

_____

_____

_____

_____

_____

_____

WEEK 2, DAY 5

Romans and Our World Today

When we consider the issues that faced the church in Rome, Romans 8:18–39 can become the lens through which we see ourselves, our world, and how God works in our world today.

1. Where do we see the damage of sin most in our world today?

We suffer injustice and see corruption in the decisions of the powerful. We feel pain from sickness and suffer loss from the companions of sickness and death. When a powerful few take economic advantage of others, creation groans in response. When water supplies are tainted and devastation is left in the wake of a powerful corporation, redemptive action is needed. When drugs race through a community or a nation, the collective sound of pain and tragedy emanating from those affected is the groan of a creation needing to be freed from its bondage. Sin devastates more than just me. It has diminished the world. When the world groans, we inevitably groan with it. We groan because we see the results of sin being played out. We groan because we are impacted by a world devastated by sin, selfishness, and greed. We live in the communities that are abused, oppressed, and left behind in sin's wake.

Following the above example, answer these questions about how we can understand ourselves, our world, and God's action in our world today.

2. Where in the past or present has the work of the church changed and restored the world?

3. How can God use pain and tragedy for the good? Does this mean it will always be experienced as good by those who are victimized?

_____

_____

_____

_____

_____

_____

4. When can it be easy to doubt that God loves and cares for us?

_____

_____

_____

_____

_____

_____

5. Why are assurances of God's love powerful in the life of the believer?

_____

_____

_____

_____

_____

_____

_____

Invitation and Response

God's Word always invites a response. Think about the way the themes of the Holy Spirit's intercession, God's great love for us, and God's desire to change the world speak to us today. How does Romans 8:18–39 invite us to respond?

The concept of being predestined is not about God selecting a group of people but about the way God has planned in advance how God plans to act and how purposefully God brings that plan to pass. God knows what he wants to do and has given us the Son to accomplish it. In a world that is impacted by the power of sin, the church works toward the liberation of people from every walk of life—but we also look forward to a change in our world.

What is your evaluation of yourself based on any or all of the verses found in the latter half of Romans 8?

Our God is not impersonal or detached.

ROMANS 9–10

Romans 9–10 is a section of Scripture that people often misread because they try to apply modern sensibilities to an ancient context. Any time we do this with Scripture, we run the risk of misinterpretation and misunderstanding the author's meaning. Our goal this week will be to decipher what Paul was really saying when he wrote these words.

These chapters were written to address questions about whether the Jews were still God's chosen people. If the gentiles could come to faith through Christ and the Jewish Christians were not "needed" to mediate God's blessing, then what role did they play in the church and as God's people? This feeling of abandonment and seeming loss of status led many Jews and Jewish Christians to reject Christ, resulting in Paul's mournful words in these chapters.

42

WEEK 3, DAY 1

Absorb the passage in Romans 9–10 by reading it aloud several times until you become familiar with its verses, words, and phrases.

WEEK 3, DAY 2

The Setting

The entire letter to the Romans has dealt with the cultural issues that faced the early church in Rome and elsewhere. The church had to move forward with the early Jewish believers and newer gentile believers united in mind and purpose. The Jews were the first people to believe in Jesus, and they solely comprised the church for the first fifteen years after the resurrection. Largely due to the life and ministry of Paul, the gentiles responded well to the gospel message and were quickly becoming the majority representation of the church. The basic situation of the first-century church was that the Jews had largely started to reject Christ, while gentiles were streaming in. What did this mean for the future of the Jews?

The Message

Paul has been arguing meticulously throughout Romans, navigating the issues of sin, redemption, and the law. Paul said the Jews did not have special advantages in the church, even though they had the law. He argued that the purpose of the law was to identify sin and not to make anyone righteous. Since Jews could not be made righteous by the law, the law had the same role for Jew and gentile alike. Because of Christ, Jew and gentile could both be declared righteous through faith. The next logical question would have been, "Is there no special role for the Jews any longer?" Paul established that each individual comes to Christ through the same faith, but there lingered an identity question. Paul spent most of his life zealously defending the Jewish faith, proud of his heritage. There were probably a few Jewish believers in the Roman church who shared his pride. More than a few of his readers probably wondered if Paul saw any role for the Jews after reading his words. Was God done with the chosen people? Paul is going to deal with this difficult question now.

To discover the plot of Romans 9-10, let's divide the passage into seven sections. **Summarize the general message or theme of each section (following the pattern provided for verses 1–5).**

43

1. Romans 9:1–5

Paul's pride in his heritage is clearly seen in these first five verses of chapter 9. He loves his fellow Jewish siblings and the religion and faith they have shared for so long. He understands their feeling of abandonment by God, yet he also laments their failures to be the people God wanted them to be.

2. Romans 9:6–9

_____
_____
_____
_____
_____
_____
_____
_____
_____
_____

3. Romans 9:10–18

_____
_____
_____
_____
_____
_____
_____
_____
_____
_____

4. Romans 9:19–29

5. Romans 9:30–10:4

6. Romans 10:5–13

7. Romans 10:14–21

WEEK 3, DAY 3

What's Happening in the Passage?

As we read through these passages there are certain ideas and words that were familiar to the original readers but are not as familiar to us. Two thousand years and a vastly different culture obscure some of these ideas from us today. You may encounter some of these words and ideas in your study today. Some of them have been explained in more detail in the **Word Study Notes** below. If you want even more detail you can supplement this study with a Bible dictionary or commentary.

Create your own brief summary or description of the reality portrayed in verses 1–5.

1. Romans 9:1–5[1, 2, 3]

_____

_____

_____

_____

_____

_____

_____

_____

_____

_____

_____

_____

_____

_____

_____

WORD STUDY NOTES #1

[1] The pride Paul has for his Jewish heritage is apparent as he lists all the blessings and advantages that have come to the world through his people. Their role has been crucial.

[2] Because of their chosen status, the Jews had every opportunity to recognize the Messiah who came to the world through their own heritage.

[3] What breaks Paul's heart is that his own people have largely rejected Christ. The family through whom God chose to reveal himself turned their back on the one who offers redemption and life.

WORD STUDY NOTES #2

[1] The entirety of Paul's argument in Romans revolves around the Abraham/Isaac/Ishmael story. Both Isaac and Ishmael are biological sons of Abraham. Even though Ishmael was the oldest son of Abraham, he was not the son of the promise. This reference underscores Paul's point that even though the Jews are older in the faith, the gentiles are also part of the promise.

WORD STUDY NOTES #3

[1] Paul's evoking of the Jacob/Esau story is intentional. God's decision to work through Jacob even though Esau was entitled to the birthright was not the natural order. With Jacob as their patriarch, the Jewish people were the recipients of God working outside the expected order. Making the gentiles beneficiaries of God's grace is another example of God working outside expected boundaries. Paul is asking: how can Jewish believers take pride in their own history of God's unexpected work while standing in the way of God working through the gentiles now?

2. Romans 9:6–9

A critic might look at this state of affairs and make the charge that God has failed. How can God be redeeming a world when the people closest to his historical effort have turned their backs to him? Paul's answer flows straight from Israel's rich history. He tells the readers that the descendants of Abraham are not limited to those who are physical descendants. The true descendants are descendants of the *promise* God made to Abraham, not just biological descendants. Those who share Abraham's faith in God are Abraham's descendants. Paul's readers would've remembered the story from Genesis about how Abraham and Sarah tried to take God's promise into their own hands, resulting in the birth of Ishmael by Hagar, who was not the promised son. Isaac, born by Sarah, was the promised son.[1] Since the promise to Abraham created the stipulation that he would be the father of many nations, Paul wants to remind his readers that the gentiles are part of the promise.

3. Romans 9:10–18

This is one of the most misunderstood passages in all of the New Testament. Through the years it has been used as the classic text in support of the idea that God has chosen a select group of people for salvation. The basic argument is that God picked Jacob based on nothing that Jacob did, and God selects people now for the same reason. Therefore, God will have mercy on whomever God chooses, and humanity has nothing to do with the process. This reading ignores not only the text but also the historical situation Paul is addressing in Romans. There was a group of people claiming special relationship with God that resulted in special privileges. Paul has already spent considerable time refuting this idea. For Paul there are no people who possess a special, inside track to God. God seeks people from every tribe and nation. When Paul states that Jacob was selected before birth, his point is that he did nothing to merit his selection—just like Abraham.[1] Paul continues to make the point in verse 17 that God has a specific purpose by reminding readers about Pharaoh in Exodus. God uses Pharaoh so God "might be proclaimed in all the earth." Paul is talking to people who claimed that only Israel was to be delivered. Paul is arguing that God used Pharaoh so the whole earth might know about Israel's God. The gentiles are now also recipients of righteousness.

4. Romans 9:19–29

We must not make the mistake of interpreting this chapter in a way that removes our free agency. Paul is well aware of the eternal danger that exists when humanity resists God's offer of grace. The biggest consequence might be that God will simply honor our choice to reject him. Nowhere in this chapter does Paul state that our rejection is predetermined in any way. Paul does say in verses 22–23 that God can use our rebellion to accomplish a larger redemptive purpose. The gentiles, formerly objects of wrath in Romans 1–8, are now part of God's people due to God's mercy.

5. Romans 9:30–10:4

This section perfectly expresses the situation Paul is struggling to understand. How can it be that the gentiles have obtained a righteousness they never pursued while the Jews are not taking advantage of this righteousness despite chasing after righteousness through the law for centuries? Paul has returned to his declaration that the law does not bring righteousness and that chasing after righteousness through the law is attempting to earn it through works rather than faith.[1] Paul desires that no one find their identity in the law anymore, and instead have Christ be the focal point of their identity.

6. Romans 10:5–13

At this point Paul goes back to Deuteronomy 30 and makes a simple argument. There is a righteousness that is available for everyone, and it comes by faith. If we confess that Jesus is Lord and believe that he is risen, then we are saved. This faith is available for all—Jew and gentile—and "there is no difference." In Paul's world, Jews and gentiles comprise the entirety of humanity.

WORD STUDY NOTES #5

[1] Remember that Paul's use of the word "works" is not about doing good deeds. Paul is referencing certain things Jews did to maintain their identity as God's people, like keeping food laws, circumcising their male children, and keeping certain ceremonial obligations.

7. Romans 10:14–21

Paul's heart is breaking over the failure of many Jews to believe that Jesus is the Messiah who rose from the dead. There is a conundrum for Paul. Jew and gentile alike have equal access to righteousness by faith, but many Jews have rejected this possibility. When Paul comes to a point of confusion he usually turns to Jewish Scripture for an answer. In verse 18, Paul uses Psalm 19 to admit that the Jews have heard the message. Then Paul begins to see a way forward for his own people, and the hope flows from his beloved Hebrew scriptures. Perhaps all hope is not lost. In verses 19 and 20, Paul uses Deuteronomy 32 and Isaiah 65 to show that the belief of the gentiles was prophesied and might be used by God for the redemption of Israel. Still, the reason for unbelief rests squarely on his own people. Paul ends chapter 10 in hope. Even though they may not believe now, God continues to be patient. His mercy will not be set aside because of unbelief.

Discoveries

Let's summarize our discoveries from Romans 9–10.

1. Abraham's descendants and all those who are invited to be part of the family of God (i.e., everyone) are descendants of the promise, not of biology.

2. We worship a God who chooses mercy.

3. Our identity should be in Christ, not in ourselves or in what we do.

4. We worship a God who is unendingly patient.

WEEK 3, DAY 4

Unbelief and the Story of God

Whenever we read a biblical text, it is important to ask how the text we are reading relates to the rest of the Bible. Romans 9 and 10 are not the only places in the Bible where unbelief is a core issue. **In the space provided, write a short summary of what each passage has to say about unbelief.**

1. Genesis 28:10–22

_____

_____

_____

_____

2. Exodus 3

_____

_____

_____

_____

3. Jonah 1

_____

_____

_____

_____

4. Acts 9:1–19

_____

_____

_____

_____

WEEK 3, DAY 5

Romans and Our World Today

When we consider the issues that faced the church in Rome, Romans 9–10 can become the lens through which we see ourselves, our world, and how God works in our world today.

1. Why doesn't it make sense to interpret Paul's use of predestined the same way the Reformed tradition uses it?

Paul has spent a decade reaching out to the gentiles. As a result, the church now comprises

primarily gentiles. Paul has spent his energy trying to win as many "non-chosen" people to

Christ as he can, even as his own people reject Christ. Paul's ministry is about all people

coming into the church, not about making only a select few welcome.

Following the above example, answer these questions about how we can understand ourselves, our world, and God's action in our world today.

2. What religious ideas or pursuits can get in the way of simple faith in our world today?

3. Why are some so resistant to new people becoming part of the church?

_____

_____

_____

_____

_____

_____

4. Paul remarks that the Jews have not obtained righteousness despite having pursued it. How do people try to pursue righteousness or holiness today without finding it?

_____

_____

_____

_____

_____

_____

5. Paul tells his readers that righteousness comes by faith. How do we complicate this simple message today?

_____

_____

_____

_____

_____

_____

_____

_____

Invitation and Response

God's Word always invites a response. Think about how the themes of unbelief and simple faith speak to us today. How does Romans 9–10 invite us to respond?

_____

_____

_____

_____

_____

_____

_____

_____

_____

What is your evaluation of yourself based on any or all of the verses in Romans 9–10?

_____

_____

_____

_____

_____

_____

_____

_____

_____

_____

_____

_____

_____

Abraham's descendants are descendants of the promise, not of biology.

ROMANS 11

Romans 11 serves as a summary of Paul's argument in chapters 9–10. God's plan can now be seen in its entirety, and it is moving forward with one goal in mind: the eventual redemption of all people. Paul has been arguing that this redemption is not just for his people alone. There is an order to this plan.

For centuries, the Jews thought they were the sole focus of God's redemptive work, but paradoxically, the gentiles are the ones responding to grace. Gentiles are being saved, and because of their participation in the family of God, the Jews will also be saved. This salvation will be through faith and not by observing the law.

Paul's larger point is that God has not rejected God's people. This is not just a future hope because there is already a remnant who have responded, and there will be a remnant who continue to respond. The Jewish believers in Rome were among the first to respond to Christ's offer of grace. Paul has responded as well, and his prayer is that his people will fully respond by faith.

WEEK 4, DAY 1

Absorb the passage in Romans 11 by reading it aloud several times until you become familiar with its verses, words, and phrases.

WEEK 4, DAY 2

The Setting

As chapter 11 opens, Paul is still explaining an ongoing role for his people, the Jews. It would be natural to think that Paul has excluded any ongoing consideration for the Jewish people. He has already admitted that God does not show favoritism, nor does the law give the Jews any inside track to the righteousness that comes by faith. If this is the case, then the Jewish portion of Paul's audience receiving the letter to the Roman church may be wondering what will become of the Jews.

The Message

There is a personal nature to chapter 11 that is hard to miss. This letter is not just an academic exercise for Paul. He has given much of his adult life to spreading the gospel to the gentiles. He was convinced that the gentiles must be included and found the promise for gentile inclusion throughout the Old Testament. The evidence of his success was plain to see. Yet even with all of his success, Paul felt intensely the relative lack of success among the Jews. Why had they ignored the Messiah who had been promised?

Paul could not believe God was finished with the Jewish people. If God was God of the whole earth, they must still have a role in God's redemptive plan. Paul's ministry hinged on his inclusion of the gentiles, and he loved the gentiles, but his heart ached for his people. What would it take for the Jews to embrace Jesus? Romans 11 is Paul's answer to this vexing question.

To discover the message of Romans 11, let's examine divide the passage into six sections. **Summarize the general message or theme of each section (following the pattern provided for verses 33–36).**

1. Romans 11:1–6

_____

_____

_____

_____

_____

_____

2. Romans 11:7–10

_____

_____

_____

_____

_____

_____

_____

3. Romans 11:11–16

_____

_____

_____

_____

_____

_____

_____

_____

4. Romans 11:17–24

_____

_____

_____

_____

_____

_____

_____

_____

5. Romans 11:25–32

6. Romans 11:33–36

Paul is simply worshiping here, reminding his readers that God is worthy of our worship, both planned and spontaneous.

WEEK 4, DAY 3

What's Happening in the Passage?

As we read through these passages there are certain ideas and words that were familiar to the original readers but are not as familiar to us. Two thousand years and a vastly different culture obscure some of these ideas from us today. You may encounter some of these words and ideas in your study today. Some of them have been explained in more detail in the **Word Study Notes** below. If you want even more detail you can supplement this study with a Bible dictionary or commentary.

1. Romans 11:1–6

WORD STUDY NOTES #1

[1] Seven thousand was probably not an exact number but was meant to be a symbol demonstrating the completeness of God's plan and people.

60

Paul wanted to assure his readers that God has not rejected the Jewish people. His first argument was to remind them he is a Jew himself and believes in Christ, even though he spent much of his life being zealous for the law. Paul is a proud Jew who affirms the Jewish participation in the new covenant. God's people were now far larger than any ethnic identity. God's people includes everyone who comes to Christ through faith. For those Jewish believers feeling isolated, Paul reached back to the familiar story of God assuring Elijah of the seven thousand to encourage these believers.[1] Their situation is not hopeless because there is a remnant who have been chosen through grace. If Israel was originally chosen by grace, then God is still able to select people through grace alone. God is free to lavish grace on whom he chooses, whether Israel and Abraham, or Jews and gentiles.

2. Romans 11:7–10

Paul wanted to be sure he was being clear, so he asked the rhetorical question in verse 7, "What then?" God's grace was exhibited in that the gentiles obtained righteousness even though they did not pursue it. The Jews failed to obtain righteousness even though they zealously pursued it through the law. Their error did not exclude them from the family of God; it merely required correction, which was what Paul was trying to do. Paul explained that their ethnically defined pursuit of the law blinded many of them to God's offer of grace but that their unbelief was the very thing being used by God for the gentiles to fully become part of God's people.

3. Romans 11:11–16

The Jews were active agents in their own unbelief, but Paul said there was no reason to think they had no hope for recovery. Every part of their resistance to grace (what Paul called their transgression)[1] was used by God for a greater purpose—namely, the inclusion of the gentiles in God's larger plan of salvation. The resistance of the Jews resulted in riches for the gentiles. Paul hoped the great success of the gentile inclusion would lead the Jews to even greater future inclusion. The greatness of grace brings plenty to both Jew and gentile.

4. Romans 11:17–24

Paul is speaking to the gentiles in this section (he made that clear in verse 13). He compares the Jews to an olive tree[1] and the gentiles to a wild shoot that has been grafted into the tree and now shares the tree's life and benefits. Paul admits that many of the branches of this olive tree have been broken off due to their unbelief. God took the opportunity offered by Jewish unbelief to invite the gentiles to become part of the tree. Paul's intent with this imagery is to remind the gentiles that they participate in something that existed long before they came along. They are nourished by the deep roots God established long ago with the Jewish people. Just as Paul previously warned the Jews about acting superior, he wants to ensure that the gentiles do not come into the church with a sense of superiority over the Jews. Paul wants to be sure the gentiles understand that the church is not a *replacement* for Israel. It is the *continuation* of God's people that started with Abraham centuries earlier. In reminding the gentiles that God did not break off the branches because of favoritism but because of unbelief, Paul is urging the gentiles to remember that God can also cut them off if they do not act in line with what God wants from God's people. This is not a warning meant to cause fear but a simple recognition that God is the judge and treats us fairly. Paul ends this section with a note of hope. The fall of Israel is not final. If Israel comes to belief, God is able to graft them in once again.

WORD STUDY NOTES #3

[1] In verse 11 the word translated as "transgression" is the Greek word *paraptoma*. It means a deliberate misstep. The Jews were responsible for their rejection of grace.

WORD STUDY NOTES #4

[1] The comparison to the olive tree is consistent with Old Testament imagery, so it is a simile that will be familiar to the recipients of the letter.

WORD STUDY NOTES #5

[1] When Paul states that all of Israel will be saved, he certainly does not mean every single individual will be redeemed. "All Israel" should be read as a parallel to "the full number of gentiles." In both, Paul sees a large number as representing the whole community. Individuals are not absolved from their own responsibility in participation with Christ.

5. Romans 11:25–32

Paul's argument has come full circle. In verse 7, Paul said Israel strived for a righteousness it did not obtain because it sought righteousness through observing the law. In verse 26 he assures his readers that Israel's rejection of Christ will only serve to bring about their inclusion later on.[1] Paul's full argument throughout Romans has finally reached a clear end point. In 1:16 Paul defined the gospel as salvation for both Jew and gentile. In recent chapters the promise of salvation for the Jews seemed like a distant hope. Here at the end of chapter 11, Paul has described the manner in which his people will believe. Just as gentile unbelief in the past has not stopped their full inclusion in the church, neither will Jewish unbelief now preclude their inclusion at a coming time. A key point of Paul's argument is found in verse 32. There are still many today who read this passage as supportive of the idea that God has predestined some people for salvation while at the same time selecting others for damnation. This flies directly in the face of what Paul explicitly states. Throughout Romans, the greatness of God's plan is the salvation of *all* people. Early in Romans Paul made the point that the law condemned all humanity for sin. There is no favoritism. If all are not made aware of their sinful state, they would never know their need for the great mercy God offers to everyone.

Create your own brief summary or description of the reality portrayed in verses 33–36.

WORD STUDY NOTES #6

[1] In verse 34 Paul is quoting the rhetorical question posed in Isaiah 40:13. The obvious answer is "no one."

[2] In verse 35 Paul is referencing Job 41:11, again asking a rhetorical question whose obvious answer is again "no one."

6. Romans 11:33–36[1,2]

_____

_____

_____

_____

_____

_____

_____

_____

Discoveries

Let's summarize our discoveries from Romans 11.

1. Paul is disappointed in the unbelief of many of his fellow Jewish people, but he is also adamant that the readers of his letter understand that they have not blown their chance to be part of God's people.

2. Paul's disappointment in his fellow Jews is mitigated, perhaps even overshadowed, by his enthusiasm for the inclusion of the gentiles in God's plan of salvation.

3. Ultimately, Paul hopes in and for the salvation of all humanity, urgently believing that all will eventually turn toward God and be saved.

4. We serve a God of great mercy who forgets our sins and welcomes us home the moment we repent and believe.

WEEK 4, DAY 4

Grace and the Story of God

Whenever we read a biblical text, it is important to ask how the text we are reading relates to the rest of the Bible. Romans 11 is not the only place where God's blessing for those who have faith, regardless of their background, is apparent. **In the space provided below, write a short summary of what each passage has to say about the role of faith or hope in the life of a person who follows God.**

1. Genesis 12:1–9

_____

_____

_____

_____

_____

_____

_____

_____

2. Daniel 12

_____

_____

_____

_____

_____

_____

_____

_____

_____

_____

_____

3. Jeremiah 31:23–34

4. Galatians 3:19–4:6

WEEK 4, DAY 5

Romans and Our World Today

When we consider the issues that faced the church in Rome, Romans 11 can become the lens through which we see ourselves, our world, and how God works in our world today.

1. How common is it for some in the church today to feel superior to others?

When new believers are welcomed into the church, they always bring new attitudes,

perspectives, and expectations. The temptation for those who have been around for decades is

to bristle at any hint of change. New believers can also be tempted to look at older believers

with skepticism and dismiss them as relics who live in a world that no longer exists. Paul

would condemn both attitudes.

Following the above example, answer these questions about how we can understand ourselves, our world, and God's action in our world today.

2. How can the biblical stories of God speaking with people in isolation and reminding them they are not alone help believers today?

3. Can you think of a time when God has used a tragedy or negative event to accomplish something good? Does this mean God *planned* for the painful event to happen?

_____

_____

_____

_____

_____

_____

_____

_____

_____

_____

4. If God's plan from the beginning was for the whole world to hear the gospel, then how should we view the idea that there exists a predestined group for whom Christ died?

_____

_____

_____

_____

_____

_____

_____

_____

_____

_____

_____

Invitation and Response

God's Word always invites a response. Think about the way the themes of God's grace and God's ultimate plan for the redemption of all humanity speak to us today. How does Romans 11 invite us to respond?

_____

_____

_____

_____

_____

_____

_____

What is your evaluation of yourself based on any or all of the verses in Romans 11?

_____

_____

_____

_____

_____

_____

_____

_____

_____

_____

_____

_____

_____

We serve a God of great mercy who forgets our sins and welcomes us home the moment we repent and believe.

ROMANS 12

Paul has completed his main argument, and it has left the Jewish and gentile believers on equal ground. We take this reality for granted today, but in the first century there was a real divide.

If Paul's view had not triumphed, Christianity would have remained an isolated sect of Judaism. If the gentiles had been forced to observe the law, then new Christians would have been forced to become Jewish first. These distinctions would have absolutely undermined Christ's command to make disciples of all nations, and it took a zealous Jew named Paul to see it.

If this new life is available for everyone now, what is our response to this offer of grace? If we are made righteous by faith, what does a righteous life look like in practice? In chapter 12, Paul starts to describe this righteous life to his readers.

WEEK 5, DAY 1

Absorb the passage in Romans 12 by reading it aloud several times until you become familiar with its verses, words, and phrases.

WEEK 5, DAY 2

The Setting

Chapter 12 begins the section of an ancient letter called the *paraenesis*. A *paraenesis* is a section of practical instruction that takes into account everything that has been said up to this point and gives advice on how to act based on what has been said. Paul has spent the entire letter engaged in a deep and complicated argument about how sin destroys individuals and how Christ and the Spirit offer new life. At the same time, Paul has also explained that sin equally degrades Jews and gentiles and that Christ offers righteousness to all equally. What may be new to Paul's audience is hearing that this righteousness comes by faith and not by observing the law.

The Message

We cannot read chapter 12 without keeping in mind everything that has come before. Every successive point Paul makes in Romans is intricately connected to what he has already said. Chapter 12 is the beginning of Paul's advice to the believers on how they should live in light of the gospel and in light of everything Paul has illuminated up to this point. Although it is our tendency in the modern Western world to approach our faith individually, it is important to remember that Paul is advising the church as a body. Our redemption story is exemplified best in how we relate to others. Life in the Spirit is never lived in isolation. It is a communal life driven by love. This love is expected to be the constant expression within the Christian church. To discover the message of Romans 12, let's examine the passage by dividing it into five sections **Summarize the general message or theme of each section.**

1. Romans 12:1–2

2. Romans 12:3–8

3. Romans 12:9–13

4. Romans 12:14–16

5. Romans 12:17–21

WORD STUDY NOTES #1

[1] The Greek word *parastesai*, which means "to offer" or "to present," is in the aorist tense, indicating a decisive moment that will have continuing effects for a lifetime. This is no on-again, off-again vision of the Christian life. This complete offering of ourselves is what is pleasing to God.

[2] The word "holy" should be understood in the sense that we have been set apart and belong to God. Now that we wholeheartedly belong to God, we can be transformed into God's likeness.

[3] The root Greek word Paul uses for "transformed" is metamorphoo—the word where we get the English word *"metamorphosis,"* which should tell us what type of change Paul has in mind. He is proposing a complete change of heart. The agent of change in us is the indwelling Holy Spirit.

[4] "Perfect" is a translation of the Greek word *teleion*. This word does not describe a state of moral perfection or a life without mistakes. *Teleion* means something that is whole, mature, and being used according to its purpose. God's will for us is perfect in the sense that it is a complete and fitting goal for a believer.

What's Happening in the Passage?

As we read through these passages there are certain ideas and words that were familiar to the original readers but are not as familiar to us. Two thousand years and a vastly different culture obscure some of these ideas from us today. You may encounter some of these words and ideas in your study today. Some of them have been explained in more detail in the **Word Study Notes** below. If you want even more detail you can supplement this study with a Bible dictionary or commentary.

1. Romans 12:1-2

Because of the great mercy of God as demonstrated in the life, death, and resurrection Jesus, we are to respond to that grace through the giving of ourselves. Paul's use of "you" is plural, which tells us it is an instruction for the whole community. When we offer[1] ourselves to God, it is not just for our benefit but also for the benefit of others. In the sacrifice of ourselves, we are continually transformed and made holy.[2] Transformation[3] does not happen all at once but is ongoing and strengthened to the extent that we stay in daily fellowship with the Spirit. When we decide to ignore the prompting of the Spirit, we cut ourselves off from the power that transforms us. If we are conformed to this present world, we will slowly learn to live more comfortably within the culture of our time. Since our culture is irreparably broken, becoming comfortable in a culture should never be a goal or source of pride for a believer. We should be shaped more and more into the likeness of Christ so we can be fit for his kingdom. Our goal is always aiming for what is to come. When we allow the Spirit to work in us, we become increasingly aware of the will of God for our lives. Some seek a complete picture of the will of God in their lives so they can decide whether to yield to it. For Paul, the reward of yielding to the Spirit is the ability to discern and live out the perfect will[4] of God. Sin prevents a person from living out God's will, hiding the ability to even see what that will looks like.

Create your own brief description of Paul's words in 12:3–8.

2. Romans 12:3–8[1, 2, 3]

_____

_____

_____

_____

_____

_____

_____

_____

_____

_____

_____

_____

_____

_____

3. Romans 12:9–13

Paul begins to close chapter 12 with guidance on how believers are to interact with their own faith community. His first words here are literally "love is not hypocritical." Love must be consistent and equally applied to everyone. For Paul, love is not an emotion of passion or weak sentimentality. Love is a quality that is chosen and evidenced by action. It endlessly pursues that which is good and it takes a stand against those things that degrade and diminish. Paul also believes that a faithful community devoted to God will share its abundance of resources with those in the community who are in need. When hard times come for the church, our response should be joy, patience, faithfulness, and hospitality.

75

WORD STUDY NOTES #2

[1] Paul has already warned his readers against arrogance, so he is reminding them to proceed here in humility even as he urges them to use their unique gifts for the good of the church while never behaving as if any one gift is superior to another.

[2] Paul's listing of gifts should not be seen as exhaustive but representative of the many gifts that exist within a body. Paul is not trying to create categories of service to be universally recognized within all churches at all times. In Paul's time there was not the clear dividing line between clergy and laity that exists today. Paul envisions meaningful contributions from every member of the body.

[3] Paul starts this list with the gift of prophesying, which we can compare to preaching today. There are those who are called to proclaim God's message to the world, and this should require study, preparation, and a deep sense of responsibility. Careful preparation and study augment the message God gives.

4. Romans 12:14–16

In verse 14, Paul's attention starts to turn toward those outside the church. While it is difficult to know exactly how the church is being treated when Paul writes Romans, we know these words are written in the shadow of Claudius's expulsion of the Jewish believers from Rome and the possibility of further persecutions under Nero. The natural response is to lash out against those who attempt to do harm, but Paul's instruction is to bless instead of curse. Imagine a world where persecution was an ongoing possibility and the advice this young church receives is to pursue strangers. Paul expects the church to be different even in difficult times.

WORD STUDY NOTES #5

[1] Paul quotes Deuteronomy 32:35, "It is mine to avenge; I will repay." When we take vengeance into our own hands, we not only diminish the testimony of the church, but we also errantly place ourselves in the role of God.

5. Romans 12:17–21

Paul's words turn darker in verse 17 as the potential for evil is explicitly stated. This is not an academic exercise for Paul but a looming possibility this young church may face. The presence of Rome lurks behind these words. The potential threat to the church is real. If the world turns on the church, Paul urges the church to respond in a drastically different way than the world might expect. Don't repay evil with evil, make every effort to live in peace, and do not give in to the spirit of revenge. Even in trial, the church's first responsibility is not self-preservation but to live the gospel in the face of violence. Paul's words are not meant to let the world off the moral hook but are instead a call to trust in God. We do not lash out in response because God is the one who ultimately holds people to account.[1] There is nothing in Romans to suggest that doing good in the face of evil is easy—of all people, Paul understands that acutely. The call to doing good in difficult situations is hard, which is why we need the daily presence of the Holy Spirit.

Discoveries

Let's summarize our discoveries from Romans 12.

1. Paul's instructions are meant to be applied communally, not just individually.

2. We can only be transformed if we are open to the ongoing working of the Spirit in our lives.

3. Spiritual gifts are various, numerous, do not exist in a hierarchy of importance, and are given by God to us for humble service to the church.

4. The church is called to live in a way that looks distinctly different from the way the world lives.

5. Evil and enemies are real, but the people of God are always called and expected to respond in love.

WEEK 5, DAY 4

Instructions for Living and the Story of God

Whenever we read a biblical text, it is important to ask how the text we are reading relates to the rest of the Bible. Romans 12 is not the only place in the Bible where God's people are given specific instructions on how to live in a hostile culture. **In the space provided, write a short summary of how these other passages address the issue of how God's people should live in the world.**

1. Exodus 20:1–17

_____

_____

_____

_____

_____

2. Deuteronomy 6:4–9

_____

_____

_____

_____

_____

3. Deuteronomy 10:16–22

_____

_____

_____

_____

_____

4. Jeremiah 7:1–11

_____

_____

_____

_____

_____

_____

_____

_____

5. Matthew 5:1–16

_____

_____

_____

_____

_____

_____

_____

_____

6. Matthew 25:31–46

_____

_____

_____

_____

_____

_____

_____

_____

7. John 15:1–17

_____
_____
_____
_____
_____
_____
_____
_____

8. Ephesians 4:1–5:2

_____
_____
_____
_____
_____
_____
_____
_____

9. James 1:19–27

_____
_____
_____
_____
_____
_____
_____
_____

WEEK 5, DAY 5

Romans and Our World Today

When we consider the issue of faithful living in Scripture and in our world, Romans 12 can become the lens through which we see ourselves, our world, and how God works in our world today.

1. Why should we take care to practice our faith in community?

Paul's emphasis in his instructions is explicitly communal. This is not a call to a solitary

existence where a believer heroically stands alone. Instead, it is a call to stand together as a

church. We must learn to depend on one another and trust other voices within the fellowship.

We become more aware and sensitive by listening to the wisdom and spiritual advice of

others. We also model our faith by how we love and treat others in our daily lives.

Following the above example, answer these questions about how we can understand ourselves, our world, and God's action in our world today.

2. What comes to mind when you hear the word "holy"?

_____

_____

_____

_____

_____

3. If we consider "worship" to be the totality of our lives, how does our approach to the faith change?

_____

_____

_____

_____

_____

_____

4. What gifts do you personally have that God could use in the communal life of the church?

_____

_____

_____

_____

_____

_____

_____

_____

_____

_____

_____

5. How is our culture turning hostile to Christianity today? How does our response to culture align with or differ from Paul's vision and ideals?

_____

_____

_____

_____

_____

_____

_____

_____

_____

_____

_____

_____

Invitation and Response

God's Word always invites a response. Think about the way the themes of holy living and practicing our faith in community speak to us today. How does Romans 12 invite us to respond?

We should remember that culture always has an impact on the people who live in that culture.

Unless Christians actively stand in opposition to the culture of the world, we will be carried

along with it. When Paul talks about "true worship," he isn't talking about Sunday morning.

Worship is what happens on Sunday morning but also Thursday evening and Tuesday during

the day. Worship is how we live our lives in each moment, when others are looking and also

when no one is looking. God's grace is so life-altering that our fitting response is to give our

entire lives to God, and that is how we truly worship.

What is your evaluation of yourself based on any or all of the verses found in Romans 12?

> Paul's instructions are meant to be applied communally, not just individually.

ROMANS 13-14

Christians are caught between two worlds. We anticipate the greatness of the kingdom that is yet to come even as we struggle with the world that is still here. In chapter 12, Paul talked about how to live in light of the gospel. In chapters 13 and 14, Paul talks specifically to the believers in Rome about how to live in response to the Roman Empire and in community with believers of differing convictions.

How we live in response to the world around us and also in response to our fellow believers in the church are timely topics in every age, but they were especially timely in the first century. For many Christians today, the discussion of life in a culture that is hostile to Christ amounts to merely an academic exercise. In the U.S. specifically, there are certainly individuals who are hostile to Christianity, but the country as a whole—the U.S. government—is not. U.S. Christians have never experienced organized, government-sanctioned hostility in the way that Christians in others parts of the world have. There are still parts of the world today where it is dangerous to profess Christianity, and the Christians living in those areas know that the experience of the Christians in Rome was a matter of life and death. Go against Rome and you could die. Staying on the good side of the authorities not only made civic sense, but it also kept them alive. While we do not know exactly what Paul was seeing in real time, or what he saw coming, it is clear that the potential for conflict was very real. Chapter 13 is Paul's advice on how to navigate this tension.

Additionally, in chapter 14, Paul continues to battle the tensions and divisions between Jewish and gentile Christians, tackling the thorny topic of personal convictions, boundaries, whose place it is to judge others, and the importance of unity and love in any healthy, Christlike faith community.

WEEK 6, DAY 1

Absorb the passage in Romans 13–14 by reading it aloud several times until you become familiar with its verses, words, and phrases.

The Setting

Historical awareness is crucial as we read and interpret these chapters. Rome had immense power. They were the unquestioned dominant force of the first century. The Roman Empire was the most dominant power the world had ever seen. It is hard for modern Christians to comprehend the emotion of this letter because many Christians in the U.S. and western Europe today live in societies that look more like Rome in terms of exercising world power than in communities that look like the group of believers Paul was addressing.

The Message

In comparison to Rome, the church was powerless. They had no authority, and philosophically, they were the new kids on the block. No believer could demand rights, nor could they even cast a vote. They lived completely at the whims and decisions of Caesar. Paul was navigating a number of complicated issues. He knew the tenuous place of the church and the real potential that Rome could snuff out these believers' lives.

We need to remember one other point when reading Romans 13–14: Paul did not always yield to the authorities. His record of imprisonments and punishments was testimony that Paul was willing to stand against authorities when it was needed and warranted.

These chapters represent tension in the life of the church and behind the scenes. That tension still exists today. There are times when we need to live peaceably and submit to the authorities. There will be times when that will not be possible. We need to be sober and cautious in our determinations about these decisions. We need to take Paul's words seriously even as we remember his life and his own willingness to take a public stand.

To discover the message of Romans 13–14, let's divide the passage into eight sections. **Summarize the general message or theme of each section.**

1. Romans 13:1–7

_____

_____

_____

_____

2. Romans 13:8–10

_____

_____

_____

_____

_____

_____

3. Romans 13:11–14

_____

_____

_____

_____

_____

4. Romans 14:1–4

_____

_____

_____

_____

_____

_____

5. Romans 14:5–9

_____
_____
_____
_____
_____
_____

6. Romans 14:10–13

_____
_____
_____
_____
_____
_____

7. Romans 14:14–18

_____
_____
_____
_____
_____
_____

8. Romans 14:19–23

_____
_____
_____
_____
_____
_____

WEEK 6, DAY 3

What's Happening in the Passage?

As we read through these passages there are certain ideas and words that were familiar to the original readers but are not as familiar to us. Two thousand years and a vastly different culture obscure some of these ideas from us today. You may encounter some of these words and ideas in your study today. Some of them have been explained in more detail in the **Word Study Notes** below. If you want even more detail you can supplement this study with a Bible dictionary or commentary.

1. Romans 13:1–7

Chapter 13 begins with a passage that is difficult for any Christian to decipher. On the surface, it seems to encourage unquestioned obedience to any government body. It has been read this way and used throughout history as a reason to support whoever happens to be in power. Chaos and unrest are not helpful for a flourishing society. The clear and simple meaning of this passage is that Christians should not thoughtlessly disregard civil authorities. Our freedom from the law of the Torah does not extend to frivolous freedom from the laws imposed by a government. Paul further assures his readers that governments perform a divinely mandated function—the restraint of evil and malicious behavior. Life cannot flourish when chaos and disorder run rampant in a society. Since governments perform this function, they are to be obeyed and supported through the taxes these governments levy and the institutions rulers create.[1] These are the obvious reasons to submit to governing authorities, but there is another reason as well: Rome has the power to kill those who rebel against the state. Paul does not want the church to volunteer for martyrdom. Lives must be preserved for the church to survive. For these reasons, Christians must show wise deference to the government.[2]

WORD STUDY NOTES #1

[1] What are we to do when governments choose evil? When governments do evil, this section does not control our response. Christians are to use sober judgement before making the decision to disobey any authority. Our witness—and innocent lives—hang in the balance.

[2] Paul encourages a level of respect and honor toward those who govern. When we follow the minimum demands but spend countless hours demeaning the people who govern, our ability to speak to our culture is diminished. If the time comes when we must intentionally go against governing authorities, such actions should always be done with a heavy heart.

Create your own brief description of Paul's message in 13:8–10.

2. Romans 13:8–10[1]

3. Romans 13:11–14

Paul compared the greatness of Rome to the darkness of night, reminding his readers that its time is nearly over. This was a powerful statement to the believers who lived in the capital of the greatest power the world had ever seen. Many of these believers would soon face that power in persecution. The believers were looking for and expecting the imminent return of Christ, who would bring an end to all the ways the night still dominated the world. In the spirit of that expectation, believers should live "as in the daytime."[1]

4. Romans 14:1–9

Paul introduces an idea in chapter 14 that is present in some of his other letters. He recognizes that some in the church have a strong faith while others are weaker. What is surprising is whom Paul considers weak. Those who live in a greater amount of freedom Paul calls strong, and those with strong scruples about a great many things he calls weak. Paul urges the strong to bear with the weak. In Rome, this would have been a call for the gentile believers to put up with the Jewish believers and their restrictive sensibilities.[1]

WORD STUDY NOTES #2

[1] The honor/shame culture is the context behind these verses. One's status was not determined by wealth but by the amount of honor or favor that was amassed in daily life through performing favors for others and reciprocity for good deeds done for oneself. Paul says our benefactor is God. Because of the grace that has been given to us, we repay that debt by loving others.

WORD STUDY NOTES #3

[1] We live according to the day when we love each other and bear each other's burdens.

WORD STUDY NOTES #4

[1] The larger issue for Paul was not meat or circumcision but the importance of unity. Paul wants Christians to remember we do not have an individualistic faith. The world is watching how we treat one another.

Create your own brief description of Paul's message in 14:10–13 and 14:14–18.

5. Romans 14:10–13[1]

_____

_____

_____

_____

_____

_____

6. Romans 14:14–18

_____

_____

_____

_____

_____

7. Romans 14:19–23

In any church there will be strong feelings on a number of issues, and sometimes these opinions conflict. In Paul's time these opinions ran along the well-known Jewish-gentile divide about food laws and dietary restrictions. Some in the church were offended when gentiles brought pork or shellfish to a church function. After years of keeping the law perfectly, Paul had come to believe that no food was unclean—but he also had become convinced that his newfound freedom was not worth the wounded feelings of other believers.[1] The only law worth keeping perfectly is the law of love. The hallmark of the church should not be strict moral codes but wholehearted love for one another.

WORD STUDY NOTES #5

[1] Paul warns that we will have to give an account of how we live, but that accounting is in the context of our life in community. The greatest commandment really is love.

WORD STUDY NOTES #7

[1] The issue, for Paul, was not personal conviction. The issue was the threat to the unity of the church when one group felt compelled to force their convictions on others. The boundaries are up to God to judge and not other believers. Those with strong faith honor God by loving all and not forcing our convictions on others.

Discoveries

Let's summarize our discoveries from Romans 13-14.

1. Paul does not preach blind obedience to the government but rather respect of the government's divine task of preserving order and restraining chaos.

2. When a government does evil, Romans 13 is not the right passage to consult; Paul's own life and his writings in other letters exemplify the sober judgment that should be exercised when Christians determine that civil disobedience is necessary.

3. Love and unity should be the hallmarks of God's people as the body of Christ.

4. Judgment according to personal conviction has no place in a community that practices love and unity.

5. Judgment of our actions is the prerogative of God and God alone.

6. Faith communities will be held to account according to how they treated one another.

WEEK 6, DAY 4

Living in Unity and the Story of God

Whenever we read a biblical text, it is important to ask how the text we are reading relates to the rest of the Bible. Romans 13–14 is not the only place in the Bible where specific instructions are given to God's people about how to live in unity, bearing each other's burdens as we do. **In the space provided, write a short summary of how God's desire for unity is reflected in these passages.**

1. Leviticus 19:1–18

_____

_____

_____

_____

2. John 17:6–19

_____

_____

_____

_____

3. Ephesians 3:14–4:16

_____

_____

_____

_____

4. 1 John 2:1–17

_____

_____

_____

_____

WEEK 6, DAY 5

Romans and Our World Today

When we consider the issues of civil obedience (or disobedience), personal convictions, and unity in the church, Romans 13–14 can become the lens through which we see ourselves, our world, and how God works in our world today.

1. Why is determining the difference between a government that warrants our respect and one that warrants our disobedience important for Christians?

Just a few months after Romans was written, Paul was in a Roman prison because he did not defer to the authorities. We must not take unquestioned allegiance to governing authorities as the only lesson from chapter 13 but read it alongside other texts like 2 Thessalonians 1:4-10, where clear warnings are given about regimes who do evil. Christians would do well to avoid both the extreme of blind loyalty to the state and also the extreme of refusing to recognize civil authorities altogether. History is littered with abuses caused by both of these positions. We must remember that the opening verses in chapter 13 were used in the 1930s in places like Spain and Germany to urge the thoughtless support of rulers who clearly intended evil. There is great danger when Christians apply these verses without discernment.

2. Why does Paul focus so much in chapter 14 on not imposing our personal moral codes on other believers?

There are times when believers need to hear the message that we might be pursuing righteousness in a way that destroys the work God is trying to do. There will always be those in the church who hold different views than we do. Sometimes those views will be more restrictive than ours, and at other times these views will be more accommodating. There will always be people who are at varying points of maturity in their journey, and we must be patient with one another. The church should never become a debate club. The weak and the strong are all full participants in the church, not in competition. The one rule that Paul emphasizes is that all people are to be loved, regardless of whether they ever change their minds to agree with us.

Following the above examples, answer these questions about how we can understand ourselves, our world, and God's action in our world today.

3. How do governments today act to restrain evil in ways that are helpful? How do we decipher when governments overstep their ordained role and act in ways that spread evil and chaos?

_____

_____

_____

_____

_____

4. How do some Christians contribute to chaos and disorder today?

_____

_____

_____

_____

_____

5. What might Paul say to us about determining the difference between taking a necessary moral stand (whether with a government or with another believer) and needlessly causing division?

_____

_____

_____

_____

_____

6. How does the age of social media fuel our tendency toward dissension?

_____

_____

_____

_____

_____

Invitation and Response

God's Word always invites a response. Think about the way the themes of civil obedience (or disobedience), personal convictions, and unity in the church speak to us today. How do Romans 13 and 14 invite us to respond?

We still await the return of Christ, although not often with the same urgency that Paul did. We have become jaded by the number of people who have incorrectly predicted dates for this return or used this expectation for their own purposes. Even if the Lord does not return in our lifetimes, Paul's advice toward unity and how we live and behave in our faith communities is still relevant. We simply do not know when our lives will end, so living with an eye toward the world to come is always proper.

What is your evaluation of yourself based on any or all of the verses found in Romans 13 and 14?

Love and unity should
be the hallmarks of
God's people as the
body of Christ.

ROMANS 15-16

Paul spent the majority of Romans making a detailed theological argument. He wanted the church to know that God both loved the Jewish people and wanted the gentiles to be counted as God's family. If God is God of the entire world, then all believers must have equal roles in the church. Paul also talked to the church about the active role of sin in the world and urged them to walk by the Spirit in order to experience holy life. It was Paul's earnest belief that this faith is worthy of our lives and our devotion.

In these last two chapters, Paul turned his attention to practical matters. He wanted to visit Rome and greet and worship with these believers in person. Paul also wanted to commend many of the believers in Rome. Rome was a difficult place to be a Christian, and Paul wanted them to know how valuable they were to him and to Christ.

WEEK 7, DAY 1

Absorb the passage in Romans 15-16 by reading it aloud several times until you become familiar with its verses, words, and phrases.

The Setting

This has been Paul's longest letter. As was the custom of the time, Paul closed his letter with a number of personal greetings and well wishes. The volume of names that Paul listed demonstrated that the church in Rome was not small and that it had the potential to be influential. Correct theology was always important to Paul, but as he aged, he learned that relationships were even more important. Without people, the message will fall silent. As he closed the letter, Paul wanted the church to know he loved them. He also wanted them to love one another. A divided church would never change the Roman Empire.

The Message

We can learn quite a bit from studying names. When Paul closes the letter, we are introduced to familiar names like Priscilla and Aquila, and a host of new names as well. These names tell stories. We should explore whether these names tell us anything important. When we read the last chapter, we find names that represent different ethnicities and socioeconomic levels in Rome. It seems the church in Rome was diverse, a true reflection of the Roman Empire. If this young church was going to change a world, it would have to look like a cross-section of that society.

To discover the message of Romans 15–16, let's divide the passage into eight sections. **Summarize the general message or theme of each section (following the pattern provided for verses 1–6).**

1. Romans 15:1–6

The first half of chapter 15 is continuing Paul's thoughts from the previous chapter about loving others, accepting one another's differences, and maintaining harmony and unity in the church for the sake of glorifying God.

2. Romans 15:7–13

3. Romans 15:14–22

4. Romans 15:23–33

5. Romans 16:1–16

6. Romans 16:17–20

7. Romans 16:21–24

8. Romans 16:25–27

WEEK 7, DAY 3

What's Happening in the Passage?

As we read through these passages there are certain ideas and words that were familiar to the original readers but are not as familiar to us. Two thousand years and a vastly different culture obscure some of these ideas from us today. You may encounter some of these words and ideas in your study today. Some of them have been explained in more detail in the **Word Study Notes** below. If you want even more detail you can supplement this study with a Bible dictionary or commentary.

1. Romans 15:1-6

In verse 1, Paul overtly identifies himself as belonging to the "strong" group he discussed in chapter 14. He realizes there are a number of believers who still live in bondage to the requirements of the law. Until the faith of the weak members matures, Paul wants the strong to avoid needlessly antagonizing them. Paul's prayer is that those who are weak will increasingly realize we are saved by grace. Paul gives the believers a new standard for life in the church. We should not choose our actions according to our own freedom but with an awareness of the need to build up our neighbor. As followers of Christ, we no longer live for ourselves.[1] If we are to glorify God in the church, we must be unified. If we allow division in our ranks, our witness is undermined.

Create your own brief summary or description of the reality portrayed in 15:7–13.

2. Romans 15:7–13[1]

_____

_____

_____

_____

_____

3. Romans 15:14–22

Paul has now completed his explanation of the gospel message. He wanted to ensure that the mostly gentile believers in Rome were aware of their status as part of God's redeemed people, and he takes one final opportunity in these verses to drive that point home. Paul is also getting ready to share his travel plans with them, so he wants to spare the church from any notion that Paul *needs* to come to correct them in some way, like he has needed to do for other churches in the empire. To make sure they understand this is the case, he reminds them they are fully competent to teach one another. In verse 16 Paul states his primary aim in his ministry to the gentiles—that they may be sanctified[1] by the Spirit. Paul believed that the Spirit changes people and that the gentiles are a living example of this change.

4. Romans 15:23–33

At this point Paul reveals his plan to visit the church in Rome. It is a part of a greater plan to travel to Spain in the near future. On his way to the western end of the empire, Paul wants to stop in Rome and personally meet the church there.[1]

5. Romans 16:1–16

In ancient letters, the writer often concluded by sending personal greetings.[1] Paul names quite a few people. Although these names may not be familiar to us, their inclusion in Romans tells a story. The names listed here tell us that the diversity in the Roman church went far beyond the Jewish-gentile divide but represented every level of Roman society. Some of the names should be familiar to readers of the rest of the New Testament. In verse 3, Paul greets Priscilla and Aquila, the couple who befriended Paul during his stay in Corinth.[2] This couple was a potential catalyst for Paul's introduction to the Roman believers. The church met at their house, which shows that synagogues were becoming hostile to those who worshiped Christ. Throughout chapter 16, Paul recognizes and commends many women. Phoebe is called a deacon in verse 1 and Junia a fellow apostle in verse 7. It is a significant clue to us today about the structure and culture of the earliest Christian

WORD STUDY NOTES #3

[1] Paul is asking the believers in Rome to offer themselves wholeheartedly to be set aside for sacred use by God. Sanctification is completely the work of God in the life of the believer. Yet it is also completely dependent on the believer's cooperation. In this ultimate contest between the selfish life and the holy life, the self must be purposefully abandoned for holiness to become a reality.

WORD STUDY NOTES #4

[1] We know that Paul made it to Rome—we can read about it in Acts. Paul may have envisioned getting to Rome freely instead of being a prisoner, but he did realize his goal.

WORD STUDY NOTES #5

[1] Paul's letter to the Romans has the most extensive greetings found in any of his letters, demonstrating the high regard he has for many in the Roman church.

[2] Their presence in Rome tells us they were probably in Corinth as a result of the expulsion of the Jews from Rome in 49 CE. With the expulsion lifted, they apparently returned to Rome to live.

[3] A kiss was a cultural practice that signified inclusion in a family or group. Its description as "holy" could have been an attempt to avoid confusion with sexual implications.

churches that there were women in leadership. These names tell us that the promise of Joel 2:28 was being realized in Paul's churches—God's spirit was being poured out on men and women. The diversity of the church in Rome does not end with male-female equality. Urbanus was a common slave name in the first century. The name Apelles is Greek. The way Narcissus and Aristobulus are mentioned—Paul asking those in their households to be greeted—could indicate that they were slave owners. We do not know if they had personal interaction with the church, but their inclusion demonstrates how many parts of society the gospel message has already penetrated. In verse 16, Paul instructs the believers to greet one another with a holy kiss.[3]

6. Romans 16:17–20

These verses are plopped into the middle of Paul's greetings in his conclusion. Commentators have noted it as odd, and some even hypothesize that it means Paul did not write this section, but we have no evidence that tells us anything conclusive. Aside from its odd placement, if we assume Paul did write it, then what it does demonstrate is Paul's unwavering commitment to unity in the church.

7. Romans 16:21–24

Paul has offered space at the end of the letter for his co-ministers to send greetings, including Tertius—the scribe who wrote the entirety of the letter from Paul's dictation. This practice was common in Paul's writings.

8. Romans 16:25–27

Paul ends his letter to Rome with one of the great benedictions in the New Testament. His words celebrate God's plan of redemption that was proclaimed by the prophets, fulfilled by the death and resurrection of Christ, made available to all nations. This is also the way the letter began in Romans 1. Paul ends Romans as he began it—with his contention that God is God of both Jews and gentiles. God is god of the whole earth, and all people are part of his plan. There is no nation or ethnicity that is outside of God's grace, and there is no individual either.

Discoveries

Let's summarize our discoveries from Romans 15-16.

1. Unity is all important for the church because division undermines the witness of the church to the world.

2. Sanctification is wholly the work of God but requires responsive participation from the believer.

3. The example of the early churches shows us that the church of Jesus was always meant and expected to be diverse in both membership and leadership.

Sanctification and the Story of God

Whenever we read a biblical text, it is important to ask how the text we are reading relates to the rest of the Bible. Romans 15–16 not the only place in the Bible where believers are encouraged to submit themselves to the Spirit with sanctification as the goal and result. **In the space provided, write a short summary of how God's people are meant to be in relationship with the Spirit.**

1. John 14:15–31

_____

_____

_____

_____

_____

_____

_____

_____

_____

_____

2. Galatians 5:16–26

_____

_____

_____

_____

_____

_____

_____

_____

_____

_____

3. Ephesians 4:17–32

4. 1 Peter 1:1–16

Romans and Our World Today

When we consider the issues of sanctification, unity, diversity, and equality in the church, Romans 15–16 can become the lens through which we see ourselves, our world, and how God works in our world today.

1. How does Paul's discussion of "weak" members and "strong" members inform our faith practice today?

There have always been Christians with different mores and practices. We worship differently and govern ourselves differently in various churches. In a world with such diversity of practice, we should be very careful about labeling other believers non-Christian. If we love God, love one another, and claim the death and resurrection of Jesus Christ as our standard, then we should welcome all as our brothers and sisters in Christ. John Wesley encouraged all of his people to have a catholic-or inclusive-love for others. That call is still relevant in our world today.

Following the above example, answer these questions about how we can understand ourselves, our world, and God's action in our world today.

2. How can an overly sensitive, rule-based Christian life rob a believer of joy and vitality?

3. What does it mean for believers to completely offer themselves to God with sanctification as the result?

_____

_____

_____

_____

_____

4. How do we see echoes of the Roman Empire in our world today?

_____

_____

_____

_____

_____

5. What challenges does the church face when a diversity of ethnicities, cultures, and socioeconomic backgrounds worship together? How does it enhance the church's message?

_____

_____

_____

_____

_____

6. What does it mean when we see women equally praised and called apostles in Romans?

_____

_____

_____

_____

_____

Invitation and Response

God's Word always invites a response. Think about the way the themes of sanctification, unity, equality, and diversity in the church speak to us today. How do Romans 15 and 16 invite us to respond?

_____

_____

_____

_____

_____

_____

_____

_____

_____

_____

What is your evaluation of yourself based on any or all of the verses in Romans 15 and 16?

_____

_____

_____

_____

_____

_____

_____

_____

_____

_____

_____

_____

_____

Sanctification is
wholly the work of
God but requires
responsive participation
from the believer.

www.ingramcontent.com/pod-product-compliance
Lightning Source LLC
Chambersburg PA
CBHW081538040426
42447CB00014B/3415